1-00

/ Stewart

Smith / Stewart
Videoarbeiten

Kunstmuseum Luzern
1.5. – 13.6.1999

Portikus Frankfurt am Main
13.11.1999 – 9.1.2000

© 1999 Kunstmuseum Luzern, Portikus Frankfurt am Main, Smith/Stewart, Ulrich Loock

Gestaltungskonzept und Satz · Design and Typesetting

Atelier EST AG, Luzern

Übersetzung · Translation

Fiona Elliott, Edinburgh; Ulrich Loock, Luzern; Shaun Whiteside, London

Photos

Smith/Stewart

Druck · Printing

Druckerei Odermatt AG, Dallenwil

Lithos · Lithography

Repro Schicker AG, Baar

Ausrüst- und Bindearbeiten · Binding

Schumacher AG, Schmitten

Umschlag · Cover

Smith/Stewart, Vent, 1998

Printed in Switzerland

ISBN 3-267-00128-5

**Ausstellung und
Katalog**

Stephanie Smith und Edward Stewart kooperieren seit 1993 – ihre erste gemeinsame Arbeit war *Intercourse*, ein Videostück mit zwei nebeneinander projizierten Bildern. Gleich zu Beginn schon sind Themen und Vorgehensweisen präsent, die, jeweils anders, auch für die folgenden Werke eine grundlegende Rolle spielen: die Inszenierung einer Beziehung zwischen Mann und Frau mittels der eigenen Körper; die Isolation eines einfachen und genau benennbaren Handlungsmomentes und seine Aufzeichnung mit unbewegter Kamera; die Bestimmung eines Bildausschnittes, der ausschliesslich diejenigen Körperzonen wiedergibt, die für die gewählte Aktion von Bedeutung sind; Rücksichtslosigkeit gegenüber gesellschaftlichen Konventionen, Desinteresse an psychologischer Untersuchung, Einsatz codebrechender Extreme der Interaktion.

Für ihre bisherigen gemeinsamen Werke haben Smith/Stewart fast ausschliesslich das Medium Video eingesetzt. Wenn sie es aber vorziehen, ihre Arbeit im Umfeld der Performance zu sehen, wenn sie es ablehnen, sich als „Videokünstler" zu betrachten, weisen sie unter anderem darauf hin, dass ihre Werke in keiner Weise mit der Aneignung, dem Zitat oder der Weiterverwertung der kommerziellen und dokumentarischen elektronischen Bilder zu tun haben, die gegenwärtig in so hohem Masse unser Imaginäres bestimmen. Ebensowenig aber orientiert sich diese Arbeit an anderen Künsten wie dem Theater oder der Malerei.

Es zeugt von einem ungewöhnlichen Mass an Klarheit über den Horizont des eigenen Schaffens, dass Smith/Stewart als eine ihrer hauptsächlichen Referenzen einen Autor angeben, der gegenwärtig eher selten genannt wird, Samuel Beckett. Gewiss haben sie die existentielle Prägnanz gerade der späten Stücke von Beckett im Sinn, gewiss aber auch die Radikalität der metonymischen Rhetorik seiner Werke.

Das Kunstmuseum Luzern und der Portikus Frankfurt am Main freuen sich, den vorliegenden Katalog gemeinsam produzieren zu können. Die Ausstellungen in Luzern und Frankfurt hingegen sind verschieden, konzipiert im Hinblick auf die jeweiligen Ausstellungsorte. Wir danken der Fruitmarket Gallery, Edinburgh, und unserem Kollegen Graeme Murray für die Erlaubnis, die englische Übersetzung des Textes von Ulrich Loock wiederabzudrucken. Dieser Text ist zuerst im Katalog der Fruitmarket Gallery zur Ausstellung von Smith/Stewart im Jahr 1998 erschienen. Vor allem aber danken wir Stephanie Smith und Edward Stewart für ihren grossartigen, freundschaftlichen und professionellen Einsatz für unsere Ausstellungen.

Ulrich Loock, Kunstmuseum Luzern
Kasper König und Angelika Nollert, Portikus Frankfurt am Main

Stephanie Smith and Edward Stewart have been working together since 1993 - their first joint work was *Intercourse*, a video piece with two images projected side by side. From the very start their work includes themes and methods which, in a different way each time, also have a fundamental part to play in subsequent works: the dramatisation of a male-female relationship using the artists' own bodies; the identification of a simple and precisely nameable action, recorded on a motionless camera; cropping the image in such a way that it only shows the areas of the body that are important to the action in question; a lack of concern for social conventions, a lack of interest in psychological investigation, the deployment of code-breaking extremes of interaction. For their joint works so far Smith/Stewart have used the medium of video almost exclusively. But in choosing to see their work in the context of performance, in refusing to see themselves as 'video artists', they are referring amongst other things to the fact that their works have nothing to do with the appropriation, quotation or exploitation of the commercial and documentary electronic images which currently define our imagination to such a high degree. Neither does the work take its bearings from other art forms such as theatre or painting.

It reveals an unusual degree of clear-sightedness about the conditions of their own creativity that Smith/Stewart cite as their chief reference an author who is mentioned rather seldom these days, Samuel Beckett. Certainly they are thinking of the existential conciseness of Beckett's late plays, but equally certainly they are thinking of the radical nature of the metonymic rhetoric in his works.

Kunstmuseum Luzern and Portikus Frankfurt am Main are pleased to be able to produce this catalogue together. The exhibitions in Luzern and Frankfurt are different, however, conceived with regard to the different exhibition spaces. We thank the Fruitmarket Gallery, Edinburgh, and our colleague Graeme Murray for permission to reprint the English translation of the essay by Ulrich Loock. This essay first appeared in the Fruitmarket Gallery's catalogue for the exhibition by Smith/Stewart in 1998. But above all we should like to thank Stephanie Smith and Edward Stewart for the great, kind and professional effort they have put into our exhibitions

Ulrich Loock, Kunstmuseum Luzern
Kasper König and Angelika Nollert, Portikus Frankfurt am Main

Exhibition and Catalogue

Das Medium als Metapher

von Ulrich Loock

„We're really exploring a male/female relationship. That's a main concern in our work; exploring what that means, what that relationship could be, incorporating degrees of obsessive, even aggressive, extremes and transgressions."[1] Auf die Frage, warum sie Video für ihre Arbeiten benutzen, lautet die Antwort, es sei so unmittelbar und ermögliche, direkt zu sehen und zu kontrollieren, was sie machen. An anderer Stelle desselben Gesprächs sagen sie, sie untersuchten auch die Möglichkeit von *live performances*, sähen sich nicht eigentlich als Video-Künstler. Doch Video ist nicht nur ein besonders brauchbares und einfach zu handhabendes *Medium*, um Beziehungen zwischen Mann und Frau zu untersuchen. Ganz im Gegenteil dürfte die Schärfe der Arbeiten von Smith/Stewart darauf beruhen, dass sie die Video-Verbindung von Bild und Abgebildetem mit der Verbindung von Mann und Frau regelrecht überlagern: Video funktioniert in diesen Arbeiten als *Metapher* für die Beziehung von Mann und Frau. Die Darstellung mit Video ist ein zentrales und unverzichtbares Element – die Übertragung in Film zum Beispiel würde diese Arbeiten ver-

[1] Stephanie Smith and Edward Stewart in conversation with Kim Sweet, in: Smith/Stewart, *Sustain*, The Showroom, 22 November – 17 December 1995, o. P. Gag, 1996 ➤

fälschen, selbst wenn scheinbar die gleichen Bilder und die gleiche räumliche Situation hergestellt würden.

Entscheidend ist, was die Künstler in den zitierten Gespräch selbst ansprechen, die Unmittelbarkeit des Video. Grundsätzlich gleicht das Video-Bild der Spiegel-Reflexion: Es ist in dem Moment auf dem Monitor präsent, in dem das Subjekt vor die Kamera tritt. Auch wenn das Video im Unterschied zum Spiegel die Möglichkeit gibt, die Bildwiedergabe gegenüber seiner Aufnahme zu verzögern, ist doch jedes Video-Bild imprägniert mit der realzeitlichen Bindung des Bildes an das Abgebildete und umgekehrt. Realisiert wird diese Bindung durch den Blick. Durch den Blick sind Bild und Subjekt aneinander angeschlossen, und das Subjekt ist in einem zwingenden Rückkoppelungsverhältnis gefangen, ohne Geschichte, ohne Differenz. Wegen dieser Unmittelbarkeit, die im Video Bild und Subjekt miteinander koppelt, bezeichnet Rosalind Krauss den *Narzissmus* als eigentliches Medium des Video, nicht etwa den elektronischen Apparat.[2]

Die Unmittelbarkeit dieser Beziehung besagt, dass es – solange der Blick die *reflexive* Beziehung zwischen dem Subjekt und seinem Bild aufrecht erhält – keine Möglichkeit gibt, jene Abhängigkeit der Abbildung vom Abgebildeten festzustellen, welche der Bildtheorie der metaphysischen Tradition zugrunde liegt, oder sich von der Abhängigkeit von der Abbildung zu lösen. Für Narcissus gibt es keine Rettung: „Gestreckt auf den schattigen Rasen schaut er mit unersättlichem Blick die Lügengestalt und geht an den eigenen Augen zugrund", heisst es bei Ovid. Und so fleht der Liebende, als das Bild sich trübt, weil seine Tränen die Ruhe des Wasserspiegels stören: „Verweile, verlasse nicht grausam den, der dich liebt! Es bleibe, was nicht zu berühren vergönnt ist, doch mir zu schauen und Nahrung dem elenden Wahne zu geben!"[3] Tödlich ist der Wahn des Narcissus, da er an der Blickbeziehung festhält, die ihn an sein Bild fesselt: Sein Begehren bleibt in perfekter und unausweichlicher Symmetrie an das Begehren des (imaginären) Anderen gekoppelt. Gemäss Lacan ist von rationaler Erkenntnis der Bildverhältnisse keine Erlösung zu erwarten, da die „Ich-Funktion" selbst sich einer Verkennung verdankt, welche das Subjekt in „imaginärer Knechtschaft" hält: Im Spiegelstadium vollzieht sich die Ich-Bildung als Identifikation mit dem eigenen Spiegelbild – dem Bild des Anderen. Von da an ist die Identität von einem Riss durchzogen, der für andauernde Frustration sorgt. „So bringt der Bruch des Kreises von der Innenwelt zur Umwelt die unerschöpfliche Quadratur der *Ich*-Prüfungen (récolements du *moi*) hervor."[4] Diesen Mechanismus zu durchbrechen, ist Aufgabe der Psychoanalyse. Sie kann „den Patienten bis zu der Grenze der Entzückung begleiten, wo sich ihm in der Formel ‚*du bist es*' die Chiffre

[2] vgl. Rosalind Krauss, Video: The Aesthetics of Narcissism, in: October 1, 1976, S. 51 ff.

[3] Publius Ovidus Naso, Metamorphosen, Buch III, zit. nach: Barbara Bloom, *The Reign of Narcissism*, Württembergischer Kunstverein Stuttgart u. a., 1990, S. 51, 52

[4] Jacques Lacan, Das Spiegelstadium als Bildner der Ich-Funktion, in: ders., *Schriften 1*, Frankfurt am Main, 1975 (=stw 137), S. 67

seiner irdischen Bestimmung enthüllt..."[5] Lacan gibt an, welcher Weg einzuschlagen ist: „Die Kunst des Analytikers soll sich dagegen darauf richten, die Sicherheit des Subjekts zu durchbrechen und zugleich in der Schwebe zu halten, bis aus ihr die letzten Trugbilder verschwinden. Und im Diskurs soll gerade in seiner Skandierung ihre Auflösung sich ankündigen."[6] Der Weg der Psychoanalyse also führt durch den Eintritt in das „Feld des Sprechens und der Sprache" heraus aus Versklavung durch den Blick und das Bild.

Ohne nun die Arbeiten von Smith/Stewart einer psychoanalytischen Untersuchung unterziehen zu können oder zu wollen, lässt sich doch sagen, dass sie mit ihren Arbeiten Verhältnisse narzisstischer Identität durcharbeiten, die sich in den Bildverhältnissen des Video realisieren. Bevor Stephanie Smith und Edward Stewart 1993 begannen, zusammen zu arbeiten, waren ihre individuellen Werke durch ihr jeweiliges Interesse an der Sprache geprägt.[7] In ihren gemeinsamen Stücken aber bearbeiten sie die Bildverhältnisse, ohne das diskursive Feld zu wechseln.

Gewöhnlich sind die gemeinsamen Arbeiten durch die Dualität der Performer geprägt. Verschiedentlich aber ist bemerkt worden, dass ihre Unterschiede, vor allem ihre Geschlechtsunterschiede gewöhnlich kaum identifizierbar sind. *Gag* (1996) zeigt in Doppelprojektion, stark vergrössert, jeweils einen Teil des Gesichtes, bedeckt mit einem farbigen Tuch, welches dann mit den Fingern, der Zunge (des anderen) in den Mund gestopft wird, bis dieser sich schliesslich über dem Stoff schliesst und der Gesichtsausschnitt bloss liegt, wodurch nun auch die geschlechtliche Identität erkennbar wird. Nebeneinander geschieht in den Projektionen das gleiche, wie sich herausstellt, in umgekehrter Verteilung der Rollen von Mann und Frau, unkoordinierte Verdoppelung der Handlung, die einer am anderen vornimmt. Auch in *Breathing Space* (1997) läuft die gleiche Handlung parallel und unverbunden in zwei Projektionen, hier allerdings ist nur der Kopf von jeweils einem Performer zu sehen, unter einer Plastiktüte, die das Gesicht während der ganzen Laufzeit des Video verbirgt. Sie atmen unter der Plastiktüte, immer dem Ersticken nahe, einmal kommt es zu einem panischen Einziehen der Luft. Unterschiede sind weitgehend ästhetischer Art, angezeigt durch verschiedene Farben der Materialien, mit denen die Performer zu tun haben. Keine wechselseitigen Reaktionen, sondern Symmetrie, die nur im Detail gestört ist, bindet die Subjekte aneinander und lässt sie als Spiegelbilder voneinander erscheinen: Was der eine tut, tut auch der andere, was einer dem anderen antut, wird auch ihm selbst angetan. Jeder bleibt in seiner eigenen Handlung (aktiv oder passiv) gefangen. „What am I looking at? Am I actually witnessing a very private,

[5] op. cit., S. 70

[6] ders., Funktion und Feld des Sprechens und der Sprache in der Psychoanalyse, in: ders., op. cit., S. 89

[7] Ich kenne diese frühen Arbeiten nicht. Es ist aber bemerkenswert, dass verschiedene Autoren das Interesse an der Sprache erwähnen, ohne Konsequenzen für die weitere Entwicklung zu benennen.

Dead Red, 1994

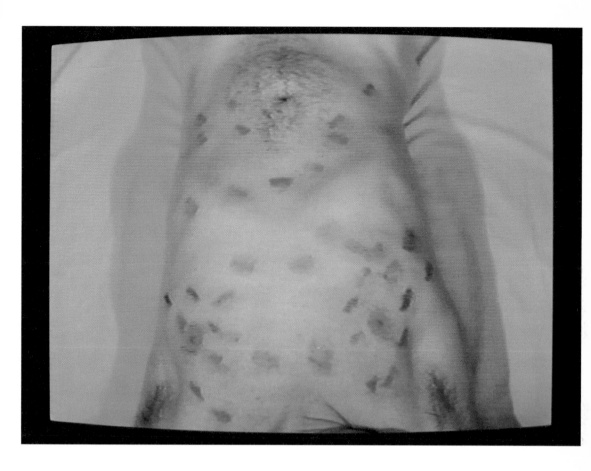

Sustain, 1995

highly aestheticized auto-erotic ritual?", fragt sich eine Kritikerin angesichts von *Breathing Space*.[8]

Struktural symmetrisch, wenn auch nicht in der materiellen Ausführung, stehen auch *Dead Red* (1994) und ein Teil von *Sustain* (1995) zueinander: Sie bedeckt seinen Körper mit Knutschflecken (mit dem Mund beigebrachte Blutergüsse), er bedeckt ihren Körper mit Kussflecken (Abdrücke von Lippenstift).

In der Arbeit *Dual* (1997), einer Arbeit mit nur einer Projektionsfläche, sind die beiden Performer ausdrücklich in einen spiegelbildlichen Handlungszusammenhang involviert, bei dem ihre Identität direkt angesprochen ist: Ihre linke Hand liegt so auf seiner linken Hand und seine rechte Hand liegt so auf ihrer rechten Hand, dass ihre Unterarme parallel verlaufen. Er (Rechtshänder) führt mit seiner Schreibhand ihre Nicht-Schreibhand, sie (Linkshänderin) führt mit ihrer Schreibhand seine Nicht-Schreibhand. Sie schreibt mit seiner Hand seinen Namen, er schreibt mit ihrer Hand ihren Namen, wieder und wieder übereinander, so dass die Schriftzüge sich bald zu einem unentzifferbaren Liniengewirr angleichen. Bei beiden vollzieht sich die Schrift des eigenen Namens, Signatur der Identität, als Inschrift des anderen, und nur für einen Moment, bevor die Lesbarkeit sich auflöst, bleibt es bei der Unterschiedlichkeit der Namenszüge. Der Schein der Interaktion erweist sich schnell als Verschleierung gegenseitiger Identifikation.

Mehrere Arbeiten also konstruieren die Beziehung des einen zum anderen als Verdoppelung, die Beziehung von Mann und Frau nach dem Modell des Narzissmus. Damit wird zwischen den Personen, als Gegenstand des Videobildes, jene Beziehung realisiert, die als zwangsläufige Bindung des Videobildes an das Subjekt besteht. Das Bildverhältnis des Video reproduziert sich in der zwischengeschlechtlichen Beziehung. Dieser Zusammenhang ist umso bedeutsamer, als eine Handlung wie die in *Gag* hochgradig sexualisiert ist. Sie ergibt das unmissverständliche Bild einer phallischen, jedoch nicht geschlechtsspezifischen, da von beiden Geschlechtern ausführbaren und erduldbaren, Penetration. Dies dürfte selbst noch für die frühere Arbeit *Intercourse* (1993) gelten, die im einen Bild sehen lässt, wie ein männlicher Mund Speichel sammelt, der in den anderen, geöffneten weiblichen, im anderen Bild, gespuckt wird. Selbst wenn in diesem Bild der aggressiven Ejakulation und willfährigen Aufnahme die scheinbar natürlichen Verhältnisse gewahrt sind, ist auch hier die Konstellation der projizierten Bilder in einem solchen Mass symmetrisch, dass die Umkehrung der Verhältnisse mehr als nur eine fernliegende Möglichkeit ist.

[8] Iwona Blazwick, Polymorphous Perversity, Anthony d'Offay Gallery, 23 October – 27 November 1997, o. P.

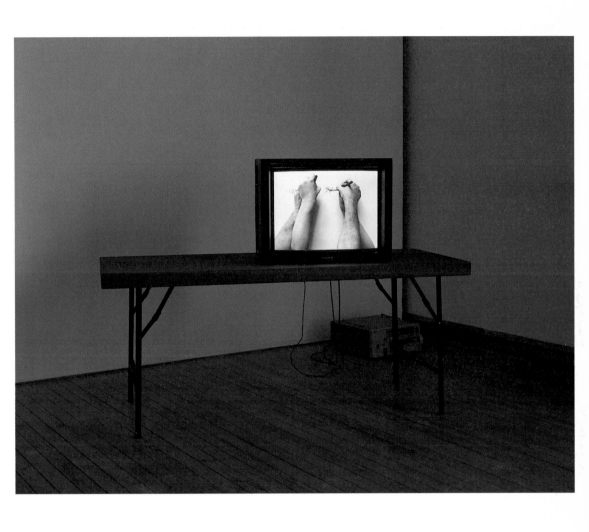

Dual, 1997

15

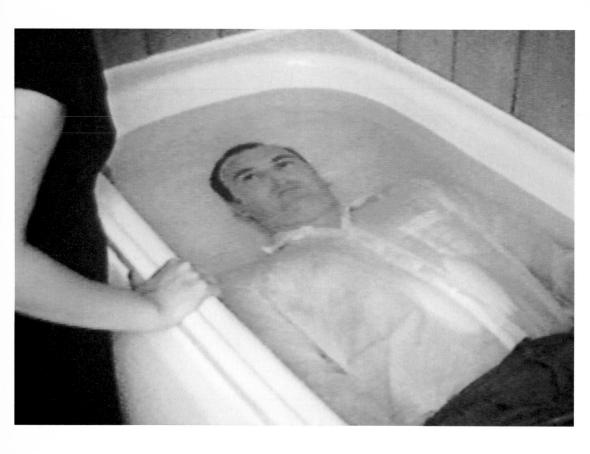

Mouth to Mouth, 1995

Andererseits lässt sich *Mouth to Mouth* (1995), in anderer Fassung noch einmal realisiert für *Sustain* (1995), als direkte Referenz auf den Narcissus-Mythos sehen, wie er im Laufe der Geschichte, verstanden als Ursprungsmythos der Malerei, immer wieder Gegenstand der Darstellung gewesen ist. Unter Wasser liegt der Mann, und sobald aufsteigende Luft-blasen anzeigen, dass ihm die Luft ausgegangen ist, beugt sich die Frau ins Wasser hinunter, um ihm ihren eigenen Atem einzublasen. Ohne zu zö-gern, wird hier der Wasserspiegel durchbrochen, der andere erweist sich nicht als Bild, das sich mit der Störung der Reflexionsfläche verflüchtigt, sondern als Anderer, der lebensnotwendig Hilfe durch eine Atemspende von aussen braucht, die ihm auch erfolgreich verabreicht wird. Die nar-zisstische Konstellation, im Mythos todbringend, ist in *Mouth to Mouth* lebenserhaltend. Doch ist der Tauchgang unter die Wasseroberfläche nicht endgültig, keine wirkliche Lösung aus der spekularen Bindung, denn sie muss, um erneut Atem zu schöpfen, auf die andere Seite zurück, wieder zur Blickbeziehung gezwungen: Notgedrungen hält sie den Blick unun-terbrochen auf den anderen unter Wasser gerichtet, um nicht den voraus-sehbaren Moment zu verpassen, in dem er wieder in Atemnot gerät. Der Durchbruch durch den Spiegel unterliegt einem Wiederholungszwang, und die Bindung an den anderen, der wechselseitig immer wieder zum Bild jenseits des Spiegels wird (der Mann unter Wasser hält die Augen eben-falls offen), bleibt der „Knoten imaginärer Knechtschaft, den die Liebe im-mer neu lösen oder zerschneiden muss" (Lacan). Und der Psychoanalyti-ker fügt hinzu, „Für ein solches Werk erweist sich nach unserer Meinung das altruistische Gefühl als eitel; wir setzen die Aggressivität ins Licht, welche unter den Aktionen des Philanthropen, des Idealisten, des Pädago-gen, sogar des Reformators liegt."[9]

In mehreren Arbeiten von Smith/Stewart bricht sich allerdings die Aggressivität, die das altruistische Gefühl, die Larve des Narzissmus, begleitet, eine eigene Bahn, sowohl in den „phallischen" Arbeiten *Inter-course* und *Gag*, als auch in den „oralen" Stücken *Dead Red* und *Sustain*. Schmerz, zugefügt durch direkte, gewalttätige Berührung der Körper, in-filtriert die visuelle Beziehung. Wenn also verhüllt aggressiver Altruismus als Signum der narzisstisch geprägten Beziehung zum Anderen zu gelten hat, lässt sich bei der körperlichen Aggressivität in diesen Stücken der Ver-such erkennen, die imaginäre Koppelung aufzulösen und durch den Schmerz den fleischlichen, empfindsamen Körper des Anderen zu reali-sieren, der zusammen mit dem eigenen Körper eingetaucht ist in dieselbe Welt. Dieser Schmerz jedoch, für den es in den Bildern selbst keinen Ort gibt und der keine Repräsentation erfährt, liegt jenseits des Sichtbaren. Es

[9] vgl. Fussnote 4, S. 70

Breathing Space, 1997 ➤➤

Ein Gespräch

(schriftlich geführt)

Ulrich Loock: Was ist die Funktion von Schmerz in Euren Arbeiten, welche Rolle spielt er bei der Interaktion der beiden Performer? Schmerz scheint auf verschiedene Weise vorzukommen, z. B. Schmerz, der nicht visuell wiedergegeben wird, den man aber aus eigener Erfahrung kennt – die Knutschflecken in *Sustain* im Gegensatz zu den visuellen Signifikanten für Schmerz in einer Arbeit wie *Interference*, wo man eigentlich nicht erkennt, inwiefern die Handlung für den offensichtlichen Schmerz verantwortlich ist.

Edward Stewart: Ich glaube eigentlich nicht, dass Schmerz eine Rolle spielt, jedenfalls nicht abgebildet, vielleicht aber Unbehagen. Hoffentlich ist dies Unbehagen psychologischer Natur – für uns und den Betrachter. Wir benutzen Ton, um das zu unterstreichen. Ohne Ton gäbe es wenig Unbehagen.

Stephanie Smith: Ich glaube nicht, dass wir willentlich Schmerz einsetzen. Doch wenn er implizit ist, so kommt das auf dem Wege der Aktion oder Reaktion zustande, wie Du sagst. (Impliziter) Schmerz soll beim Betrachter eine körperliche Identifikation erzeugen – etwa die Knutschflecken bei *Sustain* oder die gereizte Haut in den Kratz-Stücken.

19

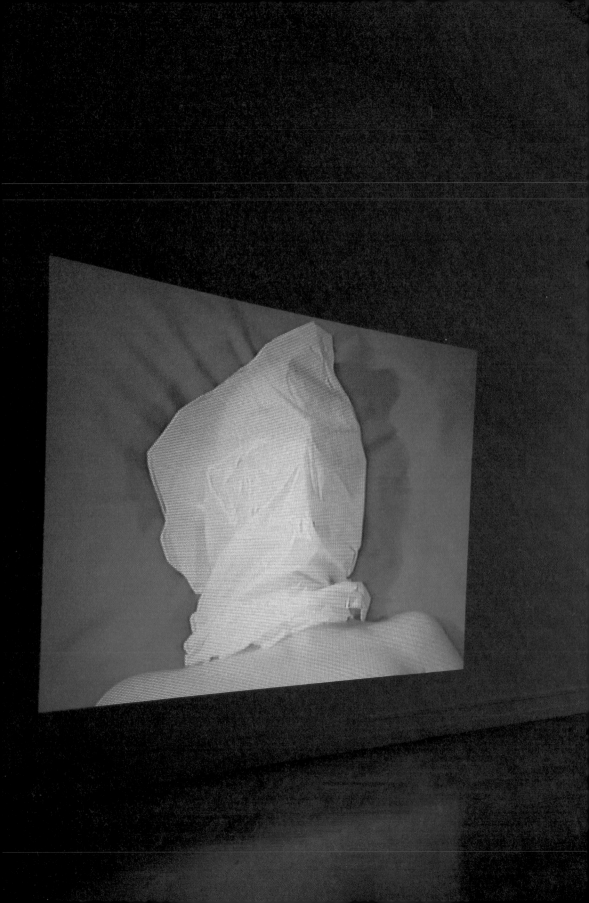

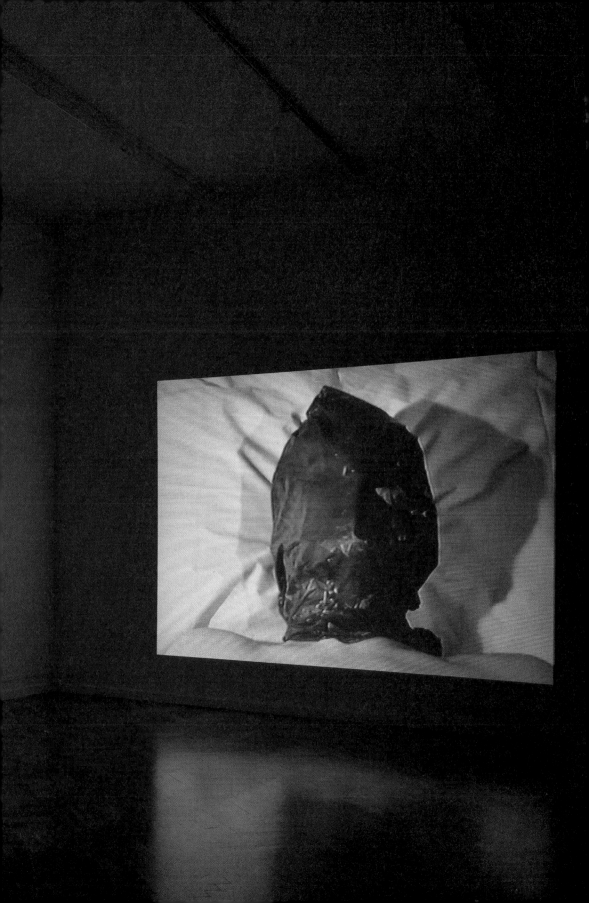

könnte sein, dass die eingangs zitierte Bemerkung der Künstler, sie untersuchten die Möglichkeit von *live performances*, genau auf diese mediale Reduktion reagiert.

In der Tat bearbeiten Smith/Stewart die narzisstische Verfassung, indem sie der Blickbeziehung zueinander zu entgehen und dem Auge seinen Status als vorherrschendes Sinnesorgan zu nehmen suchen. Eines ihrer letzten Stücke, *Inside Out* (1997), unterscheidet sich von allen anderen dadurch, dass es nicht jene Dualität der Performer beinhaltet, die bisher verbindlich gewesen war – wenn es auch sein mag, dass von dieser spezifischen Dualität lediglich abstrahiert und sie ersetzt wird durch die Gegensätze Innen-Aussen, Offen-Geschlossen oder Hell-Dunkel. Auf dem dunklen Monitor öffnet sich langsam ein Lichtschlitz, bis er mandelförmige Gestalt erreicht und der Ausstellungsraum selbst hell wird, um mit der sich schliessenden Öffnung wieder in Dunkelheit zu versinken usw. Das Bild zeigt den Blick aus der Tiefe der Mundhöhle nach aussen, erkennbar an der Bildbegrenzung durch Zähne und Lippen. Die Kamera nimmt im Mund die Stelle der Netzhaut ein, der Mund wird sehend und ersetzt das Auge, er sieht auch aus wie ein Auge.

In einem Grossteil der Videos ist es so, dass der Mund in die Blickbeziehung zum anderen eingeschoben wird, Mund-zu-Körper oder Mund-zu-Mund. In Arbeiten wie *Sustain, Dead Red* oder *Dual* stimmen Aufnahmewinkel der Kamera und Bewegung des Mundes in Richtung des Körpers des anderen weitgehend überein. Damit aber bleibt die Konditionierung der oralen Beziehung durch die visuelle immer deutlich. Die Kussspuren, Blutergüsse und Abdrücke von Lippenstift, sind vor allem sichtbar, und die Penetration durch den Finger, der Stoff in einen Mund stopft, lässt sich als Bild für den phallischen Charakter des männlichen Blickes sehen. Nun aber, in *Inside Out*, gibt der Mund diesen Blick zurück. Hier ist der Mund nicht, wie bei den anderen Arbeiten, in die Blickbahn eingesetzt, sondern er ist selbst Sitz des Blickes. Was durch ihn zu sehen ist, ist weisses Licht, die Weisse des Lichtes, keine Gestalten, keine Objektivierung – es ist reiner Zufall, dass ich an dieser Stelle das Bändchen *Elemental Passions* von Luce Irigaray aufschlage und gleich auf Seite 7 lese, „White. Immense spaces. White, a rush of breath. Be swift, marry this breath. Remain in it. Make haste. Let it not abandon me. Let me not turn from it. Be swept up: my song. / You give me a blank white mouth. My white mouth, open, like an angel in a cathedral. You have stopped my tongue. What remains is song. I can say nothing but sing. / A song, for you. But that ‚for you‘ is not a dative. Nor that song, a gift. Not received from you, not produced by me, nor for you, that song: my love with you. Inter-

Ich denke, wir verstehen das mehr im Sinne von unserer Ausdauer und unseren „Rollen", d. h. im Sinne von Macht-Beziehungen, die sich verändern können, simultan oder individuell.

Der „Schmerz", auf den Du bei *Interference* hinweist, ist eine Reaktion, die unser Unbehagen zeigt, wenn uns direkt in den Kopf (vor allem in die Ohren) geschrien wird. Der Betrachter sieht nur, wie wir uns abwenden. Er hört nicht den Ton, wie wir ihn gehört haben – denn das Mikrophon befindet sich in unserem Mund und registriert daher den Lärm ganz anders. Uns interessiert diese scheinbare Trennung von Ton und Bild und die Beziehung zwischen *live* und Aufnahme. Aufgrund der Intensität und des Tempos scheint es unangenehm oder schwierig, *Interference* anzusehen. Die Eindringlichkeit bietet sich für Assoziationen an und ist als gewaltsam und sexuell verstanden worden; es schwankt dazwischen, jemandem wehzutun oder ihn zu überwältigen und ihn leidenschaftlich zu küssen und zu ersticken – jemand hat sogar gesagt, es sehe aus, als fügten wir einander Elektroschocks zu.

Auch in *Vent* gibt es impliziten Schmerz, und zwar durch den Ton erzeugt – das dauernde Gebrüll ist irgendwo zwischen Schrei und Atem.

ES: Ja, und da es im Innern des Körpers ist, verinnerlicht auch der Betrachter den Ton.

Allgemeiner: was ist die Funktion von extremen, aggressiven, Codes brechenden Verhaltensweisen in der Beziehung zueinander?

ES: Gute Frage. Wir zeigen manchmal „intime Handlungen", setzen aber Bildausschnitte ein, um den bestimmten Kontext der Handlung zu entfernen. So – und weil wir sie in der Öffentlichkeit zeigen – werden diese Handlungen extrem und aggressiv, oder bezeichnen Aggression – aber zugleich sprechen sie von Intimität, Zuneigung, Begehren und Liebe.

SS: Es ist Liebe! Es hat damit zu tun, Intensität und Körperlichkeit zu steigern. Jedenfalls sind unsere Beziehungen nicht nur aggressiv – da ist die lebenserhaltende Seite von *Sustain* (unter Wasser) neben den Knutschflecken. *Dead Red* begann mit dem Wunsch, jemanden über und über zu küssen, und das verwandelte sich in obsessive, possessive Zeichnung.

Es kann aggressiv werden, da wir uns für Desorientierung interessieren, für Extreme, für das „Dazwischen". Unsere frühen Arbeiten beruhten auf Einverständnis, hatten aber auch damit zu tun, das Vertrauen des anderen auf die Probe zu stellen. Aggression war ein unvermeidliches Element.

Gelegentlich habt Ihr Euch gewehrt, als Videokünstler bezeichnet zu werden. Ihr habt sogar über die (theoretische) Möglichkeit gesprochen, *live performances* zu machen. Soweit ich weiss, habt Ihr das aber nie wahr-

mingled. Escapes from me. A cloud..."[10] Es ist ein anderer Blick, der seinen Sitz im Mund hat, als derjenige, dessen Bild wir im Finger zu sehen meinen, der sich in den Mund hineinzwängt. Er objektiviert und identifiziert nicht, er ist umfassend, in die Welt verwickelt, körperlich.

Breathing Space ist die Arbeit, in der die beiden Performer getrennt voneinander, parallel zueinander das gleiche tun, nur eins, Luftholen unter einer Plastiktüte. Sie ringen um Atem und setzen sich Atemzug für Atemzug durch gegen die Unmöglichkeit zu atmen. Mehrere andere Arbeiten haben ebenfalls mit dem Atmen zu tun oder sind durch das Atmen bestimmt, auch wenn sie es nicht explizit zu ihrem Gegenstand haben. Das Atmen erfüllt verschiedene Funktionen. Es ist Sache des Mundes, Hauch, der sich ausdehnt und den Raum erfüllt, Verbindung von Innen und Aussen des Körpers durch Luft, die sich unablässig, bis zu einer endgültigen und unwiderruflichen Unterbrechung, in beide Richtungen bewegt, nicht fokussiert wie der Blick. Die Einführung des Atmens trägt bei zur Relativierung, wenn nicht Verdrängung des Auges. Das Atmen ist es aber auch, das Handlungen, überhaupt den Verlauf des Lebens in regelmässigen Rhythmen skandiert. So gibt es der zwanghaften Wiederholung, die wir in der Arbeit *Mouth to Mouth* beispielsweise als Spur einer psychischen Bestimmung, einer narzisstischer Bindung nämlich, gesehen haben – gerade dort, wo der Spiegel durchbrochen wird – eine natürliche und körperliche Fundierung.

Die wenigsten Videos von Smith/Stewart sind ohne Ton – eine Ausnahme ist *Dead Red*, gewiss das „visuellste" von allen Stücken. Der Ton ist gewöhnlich laut und erfüllt den Raum. Er umhüllt den Rezipienten und zieht sie oder ihn in das Werk herein, in mehreren Arbeiten ist es das Atemgeräusch. Es verbindet sich mit dem Atmen des Aussenstehenden. Wie diejenigen, deren Bilder ich sehe, so atme auch ich. Der Unterschied zwischen Sehen und Hören bewirkt, dass ich das aufgezeichnete Geräusch nicht im gleichen Mass als Reproduktion verstehe wie ein Bild.

Mit dem Atemgeräusch wird eine dritte Instanz in einer Weise involviert, die sich entscheidend von der Betrachterposition unterscheidet. Der Rezipient sieht, was die Kamera aufgenommen hat. Grundsätzlich stimmt sein Blick mit dem Kamerablick überein, sein idealer Standpunkt koinzidiert mit dem Blickpunkt der Aufzeichnung. Dabei haben die Doppelprojektionen allerdings nicht zuletzt die Funktion, die Einheit des Standpunktes in Frage zu stellen, den Rezipienten von der Verpflichtung auf einen einheitlichen Blickpunkt zu entlasten. Sodann sind Videos, in denen der Aufnahmewinkel mit der Blickrichtung des einen Performers übereinstimmt, zu unterscheiden von anderen, in denen die Kamera eine

[10] Luce Irigaray, Elemental Passions, New York 1992.

24

gemacht. Was ist der Grund dafür, dass Ihr weiterhin Video als Euer Medium verwendet?

ES: **Wir haben uns für die** *live performance* **interessiert, weil wir den Betrachter noch näher heranbringen wollten – ihn zu einem Teil der Arbeit machen wollten. Selbstverständlich haben wir immer gefunden, dass unsere Arbeit eine sehr physische Erfahrung für den Betrachter ist, aber uns begann der Unterschied zu interessieren zwischen unserer eigenen Produktionserfahrung (z. B. unter Wasser sein und auf Luft warten; unter den Plastiktüten unfähig sein, deutlich zu sehen oder zu hören, zu schwitzen, in Panik zu geraten, zu versuchen, sich zu konzentrieren usw.) und wie wir sie zeigten. Das führte uns zu einigen interessanten Fragen – wir wollten, dass der Betrachter sich unserer Erfahrung annähert. Wir finden allerdings, dass das auch bei einigen unserer neueren Arbeiten gelungen ist, vor allem bei** *Inside Out, Vent* **und** *Interference*.

SS: **Mit Video zu arbeiten, erscheint uns noch immer am besten geeignet. Wir interessieren uns für das Potential der** *live performance*, **aber es hat sich noch nicht die richtige Gelegenheit ergeben. Wir wollen die Beziehung zwischen** *live* **und Aufzeichnung verschärfen, aber vielleicht nicht mittels eines** *live* **Stückes, vor allem, da es jetzt auch mit den Video-Arbeiten selbst gelingt. Wir sind nicht „gegen"** *live performances*, **sondern versuchen, deren Möglichkeiten in das Video einzubeziehen.**

Es interessiert uns auch, Film, Photo, Ton und Raum im Zusammenhang mit bestimmten Ideen zu verwenden. Wir sind nicht an das Video gebunden, sondern benutzen das, was praktisch und konzeptionell für unsere Untersuchungen sinnvoll ist.

1995 habt Ihr gesagt, „wir untersuchen eine Mann/Frau-Beziehung." Stimmt das auch noch für neuere Arbeiten wie *Inside Out* oder *Vent*?

ES: **Nur insofern, als wir uns in einer Mann/Frau-Beziehung befinden – die Intimität dieser Beziehung ermöglicht es uns, in unserer Arbeit bestimmte Dinge zu tun, und sie wird unausweichlich in ihr reflektiert. Ich glaube, die ursprüngliche Aussage hatte damit zu tun, die Politik intimer Beziehungen im allgemeinen zu untersuchen – aber praktisch, durch unsere eigene.**

SS: **Unsere Arbeit kommt daher – das ist eine unausweichliche Tatsache! –, aber unsere Ideen haben sich weiterentwickelt, und es ist nicht mehr notwendigerweise das „Thema". Die Mann/Frau-Beziehung muss nicht spezifisch sein – sie kann über alle intimen Beziehungen Aussagen machen. Unsere Arbeit ist hoffentlich allgemeiner als unsere Beziehung. Unsere Arbeit hat jetzt mehr mit dem Körperlichen zu tun; die Arbeiten, die Du ansprichst (***Inside Out*** und** ***Vent***), beschäftigen sich mit der Vor-**

dokumentarische Position einnimmt und eine Szene unabhängig von der Bewegung der Performer rahmt. In ersterem Fall ist die Handlung so inszeniert, dass die narzisstische Beziehung zwischen Performer (und Rezipienten) einerseits und dem Bild andererseits dem Wesen des Videos entspricht, in anderen Fällen bleibt der Rezipient aussenstehender Betrachter.

In *Breathing Space* sind die aufgezeichneten, auf zwei Projektionsflächen wiedergegebenen, gleichen Handlungen der Performer völlig voneinander losgekoppelt. Der Spiegeleffekt bleibt unrealisiert, eine Art blinder Narzissmus. So ist es der Rezipient, der die Atemgeräusche beider zusammen hört und mit seinem eigenen Atmen zusammen hört.[11] Über das Atmen stellt er eine Verbindung her zwischen den verdoppelten Bildern. Diese Verbindung realisiert im Gegensatz zur visuellen Gleichheit eine tiefe, körperliche Individualität der Performer, an der sich die eigene körperliche Individualität des Rezipienten abzeichnet. So erscheint es als Funktion des umfassenden Geräusches, den Dritten, der sich nicht auf einen Betrachter reduzieren lässt, mit den Performern ins Spiel zu bringen und so diese miteinander ins Spiel zu bringen – eine Dimension, die jedoch ausschliesslich dem Rezipienten vorbehalten ist. Mit der Verwickelung des Dritten, einem Sehenden und Hörenden, einem Atmenden, wird der spekularen Beziehung ihre Auflösung angekündigt zugunsten eines existentiellen Beieinander der wirklichen Körper in einer körperlichen Welt – der Dritte ist es, der den Schmerz empfindet, dessen Repräsentation von den Videos ausgeschlossen ist. Zugleich bleibt die unüberwindliche Distanz und zwanghafte Nähe der Bildbeziehung des Video respektiert. Dieser Spiegel, den die Projektionsfläche des Video darstellt, lässt sich noch nicht durchbrechen. Völlig adäquat werden die Bilder direkt auf die Wand des Ausstellungraumes projiziert: der Projektionsschirm ist eine Mauer. So zeigen die bisherigen Arbeiten von Smith/Stewart, in welche Richtung die Reise gehen könnte, die kaum noch begonnen ist.

Was die Arbeit von Smith/Stewart bedeutend macht, ist die Rigorosität, mit der sie im Verhältnis von Mann und Frau das reflexive Verhältnis von Bild und Subjekt realisieren, welches herzustellen zum Wesen des Video gehört. An der Macht dieses Verhältnisses ist kein Zweifel erlaubt. Sie erweitern die Uneinheitlichkeit, die das Ich ursprünglich kennzeichnet und im „Stadium", dem „Stadion", einer umrissenen Zeit und eines befestigten Ortes hervortritt[12], zum parallelen Nebeneinander und Einander-Gegenüber zweier Personen. Diese beiden Personen sind als Mann und Frau identifizierbar, doch ihr reflexives Verhältnis löst die Vorgabe fixierter Geschlechtlichkeit auf. Im Innern des „Stadions" nehmen sie die

[11] Vgl. meinen Text *Breathing Space. The Third One as Medium*, in: Katalog *Glasgow*, Kunsthalle Bern 1997

[12] Lacan schreibt, „Entsprechend symbolisiert sich die *Ich*-Bildung (formation du *je*) in Träumen als ein befestigtes Lager, als ein Stadion, das – quer durch die innere Arena bis zur äusseren Umgrenzung, einem Gürtel aus Schutt und Sumpfland – geteilt ist in zwei einander gegenüberliegende Kampffelder, wo das Subjekt verstrickt ist in die Suche nach einem erhabenen und inneren Schloss, dessen Form – manchmal im gleichen Szenario danebengestellt – in ergreifender Weise das *Es* symbolisiert. Wir finden diese Strukturen einer Befestigungsanlage – deren Metaphorik spontan auftaucht, als würde sie unmittelbar aus den Symptomen des Subjekts hervorgehen – in ähnlicher Weise auf mentaler Ebene realisiert; sie markieren dort Mechanismen der Inversion, Isolation, Verdoppelung, Annullierung, Verschiebung, die der Zwangsneurose zugeschrieben werden." Der Übersetzer weist darauf hin, dass das französische Wort *stade* sowohl „Stadium" wie „Stadion" bedeuten kann, also sowohl etwas zeitlich wie etwas räumlich Begrenztes, vgl. Fussnote 4, S. 67 f.

stellung, Erfahrung, Körperlichkeit des Körpers (männlich oder weiblich, persönlich oder allgemein). Es hat eine Verschiebung gegeben.

Welche theoretische Stellung hat die Videokamera in den Arbeiten, in denen Ihr sie in den Körper hineinnehmt, um von innen nach aussen zu filmen – im Unterschied zu ihrer Position in früheren Arbeiten, wo sie mit dem Blick eines der Performer oder eines Dritten übereinzustimmen schien?

ES: **Wir haben die Kamera sowohl als Medium als auch als Teil unserer selbst benutzt, und wir tun das weiterhin. Wenn wir die Kamera oder das Mikrophon in den Körper hineinbringen, so versetzt das den Betrachter „in" uns oder ihn selbst und macht ihn zu einem Teil der Arbeit (wie schon zum Thema Performance bemerkt).**

SS: **Wenn wir die Kamera in den Körper setzen, um hinauszuschauen, streben wir eine direkte physische Reaktion des Publikums an. Der Körper selbst rahmt das Bild.**

Die Vorstellung, „im" Kopf zu sein, hat aber nicht nur mit der Kameraposition zu tun – genauso wichtig ist es, wie die Installation im Raum funktioniert. Uns interessiert auch die andere Kameraposition, die Du ansprichst, vor allem der Blick des Dritten. Bei *Breathing Space* z. B. bedeutet es etwas, wenn man auf jemanden hinunterschaut. Dasselbe gilt auch für *Black Out* – die Handkamera registriert sogar die Atembewegung des anderen, der ebenfalls eine Kamera hält – dieser „Andere" ist in der Tat auch der erste Betrachter.

Wir haben angefangen, mit der beweglichen Kamera zu arbeiten, während die Kamera vorher meist statisch war. Das kann die Arbeit weniger voyeuristisch machen, und damit ist der Betrachter stärker mit einbezogen – kein reiner Betrachter.

Welche Funktion hat das (weisse) Licht in Arbeiten wie *Inside Out* oder *Vent* (in gewisser Weise das Fehlen eines Bildes)?

SS: **Das weisse Licht ist das Unendliche, die Leere und hat mit Sehen zu tun. In *Inside Out* und *Vent* ist das Bild auf das Fundamentale reduziert – man muss kein Bild sehen –, Licht und Dunkel, Mund, Zähne sind genug. Es ist wichtig, wie das Licht im Ausstellungsraum funktioniert – das gilt vor allem für *Inside Out*, wo das Licht einen Notausgang beleuchtet. Wenn der Mund geschlossen ist, versinkt der Raum in vollkommener Dunkelheit (und Stille). Man muss auf Licht und Atem warten, um sehen (und herauskommen) zu können.**

In *Vent* ist der Ton wichtig. Die Weisse füllt die ganze Stirnwand und wird zu einem Lichtschirm. Die (grauen) Zähne, die von oben und unten hereinkommen, sind visuelle Schlüssel für die Herkunft des Tons – die Stim-

Möglichkeiten der Verräumlichung wahr, das Verhältnis zueinander zu verschieben, vor allem den Mund in die Blickbeziehung einzuschieben, bis der Mund schliesslich den Blick in sich aufnimmt und selbst sehend wird. Mit dieser Bearbeitung ihrer Beziehung aber verschieben sie das Verhältnis zwischen Bild und Subjekt des Video. Um im Bild zu bleiben, liesse sich sagen, mit dem „Stadion" werde ein neuer Ort für die Instanz des „Zuschauers" geschaffen, dessen körperliche Verwicklung in das räumlich installierte Werk, vor allem dessen Eingetaucht-Sein in das Geräusch des Atmens, mit dem er mitatmet, die Wirklichkeit der anderen Körper rekonstruiert, die im Video und dort füreinander nichts als Bilder sind.

me wird dauernd ausgestossen, nach draussen gerichtet in den offenen Raum ausserhalb, jenseits des Körpers. Unablässig.

ES: „Das Fehlen eines Bildes", das ist interessant. Wir sehen unsere Arbeit nicht nur im Sinne eines Bildes, wie im projizierten Bild. Das „Bild" ist das, was man durch die Position erfährt, die einem die Kamera anweist, durch den Ton des Stückes und durch den Raum der Installation selbst. *Inside Out* und *Vent* haben mit dem Innen und Aussen zu tun – man braucht kein anderes Bild.

Wie denkt Ihr die Beziehung zwischen Bild und Ton in Euren neueren Arbeiten (der Ton scheint jetzt eher unabhängig vom Bild als vorher)?

SS: Ton (und umgekehrt Stille) ist immer entscheidend wichtig für uns. Es ist immer der wirkliche Ton, gewöhnlich verstärkt. Das ist bis heute so, wenn auch der Ton zu etwas anderem (vielleicht ein wenig mehr „losgehakt") wird dadurch, wie wir ihn aufzeichnen. Wenn das Mikrophon z.B. in den Körper eingesetzt wird, wie für *Interference* und *White Noise*, kommt es zu Verzerrungen. Wir möchten das im Verhältnis zum Bild noch verstärken und möchten vielleicht, dass der Ton zu etwas Eigenem wird (vielleicht völlig eigenständig).

ES: Ich würde nicht sagen, dass er jetzt unabhängiger ist. Wir benutzen immer noch den wirklichen Ton der Aufzeichnungen selbst, sogar in *Interference* – wir zeichnen den Ton nur aus einer anderen Perspektive auf, indem wir den Körper als Mittler für den Ton einsetzen. Wieder machen wir das, um durch die Trennung von Ton und Bild mit der Beziehung des Betrachters zu der Handlung zu spielen.

Die Beziehung zwischen Mund und Auge, bis dahin, dass es möglich zu werden scheint, eins für das andere einzusetzen, dürfte zu den fundamentalen Strukturen Eurer Arbeit gehören. Wie denkt Ihr diese Beziehung?

SS: Diese Beziehung hat sich entwickelt. Wir haben den Mund als Forschungsorgan, beinahe zum Sehen benutzt, und die Kamera als Mittel, um sichtbar zu machen, als Sehorgan.

Der Titel unserer Ausstellung in der Fruitmarket Gallery in Edinburgh vor kurzem war *Hooded.Bared* (aus Becketts *Company*), eine Beschreibung des Augenlids, das sich öffnet und schliesst. (Wir haben auch andere Lesarten gefunden). Die engste, offensichtlichste Beziehung zwischen Mund und Auge findet sich in *Inside Out*, wo der Mund zum Auge wird. Die Mund/Auge-Struktur bezieht sich auch auf die Beziehung der Sprache zum Visuellen.

ES: Hinausschauen, damit kommen wir so nahe wie möglich dazu, den Körper als Öffnung zu benutzen – das ist der Anfang und das Ende (vor allem in Beziehung zum Atem). Er ist ein Kommunikationsmittel, prä-verbal und mit Sprache.

Eines der wichtigsten, am häufigsten wiederkehrenden Elemente in Eurer Arbeit ist der Atem (als Bild und als Ton). Was ist die Funktion des Atmens und worauf bezieht Ihr Euch, wenn Ihr den Atem so wichtig nehmt?

ss: Es ist ein fundamentaler Akt – und einer des Körpers. Wir haben den Atem sichtbar und hörbar gemacht, indem wir in verschiedener Weise die Aufmerksamkeit auf ihn gelenkt haben. Mit dem Atem machen wir den Betrachter seines eigenen Körpers, seines eigenen Atems bewusst – er wird zu einem Teilnehmer. „Der Dritte als Medium".

Atem misst Zeit, er kann Extreme erreichen (Erstickung, Atemlosigkeit). Er kann regelmässig sein oder anschwellen. Dein und mein Atem können übereinstimmen oder nicht – zusammen oder auseinander.

Man kann Atem auf sich selbst und oder einen anderen beziehen.

Atem kann Leben retten.

Uns interessiert die Beziehung zwischen Atem und Speichel – dass er mit dem Körper und seinen Funktionen verbunden ist.

Er hat mit Sterblichkeit, Anwesenheit und Abwesenheit zu tun.

Es ist ein fortgesetzter Rhythmus, ein Pulsieren vor und jenseits der Sprache.

Er ist etwas, das immer da war.

ES: Uns interessiert die Dunkelheit sehr. Ohne Licht und ohne Geräusch beginnt man, andere Geräusche zu hören – die eigenen.

Unsere Arbeit, unsere „Performances" machen uns unseren eigenen Atem bewusst, oft durch den des anderen, und wir haben versucht, sichtbar zu machen, was gewöhnlich nicht zu sehen ist.

White Noise, 1998

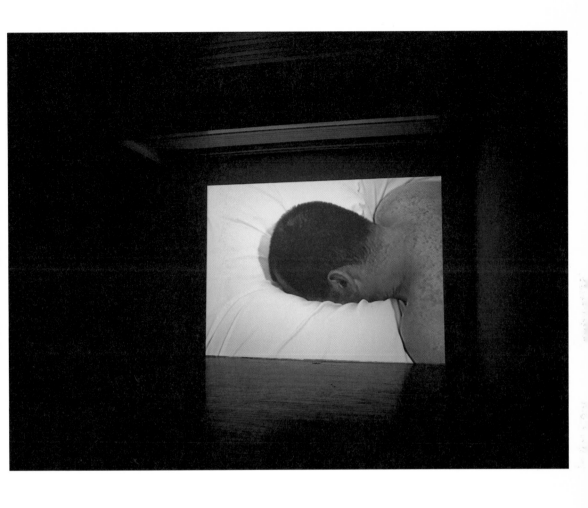

Interference, 1998

Vent, 1998

Inside Out, 1997

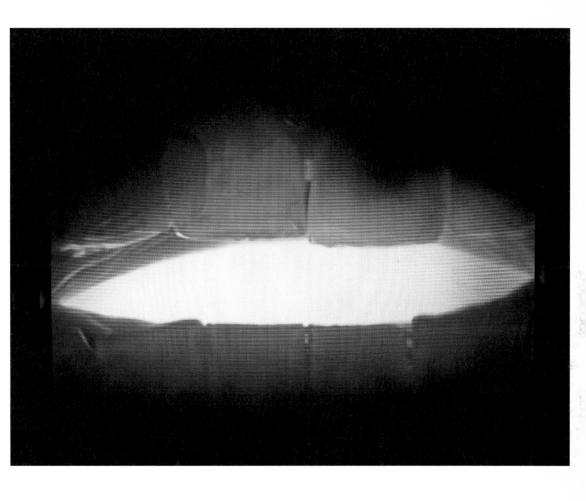

Static, 1999

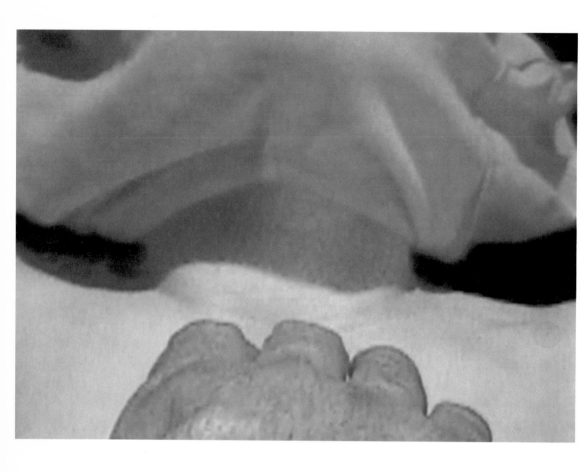

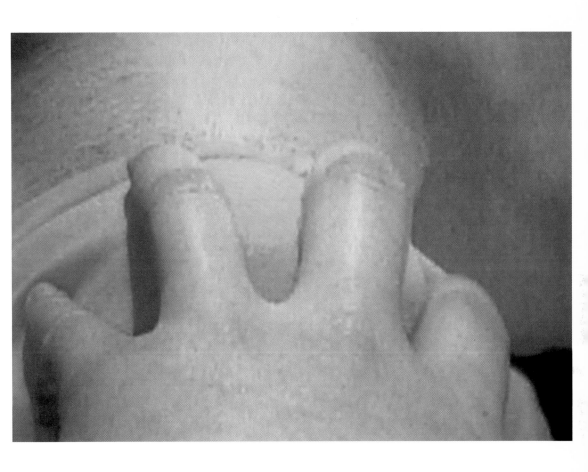

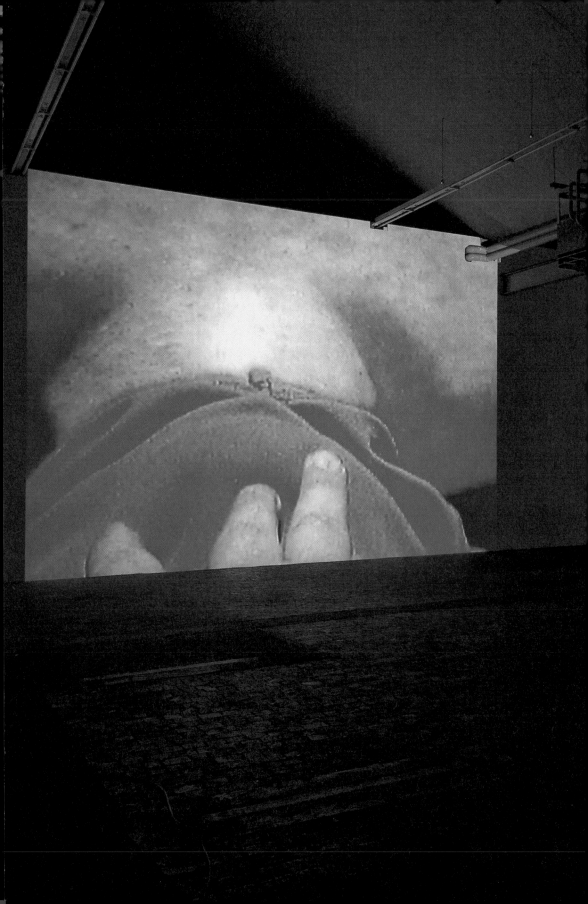

The Medium as Metaphor

by Ulrich Loock

"We're really exploring a male/female relationship. That's a main concern in our work; exploring what that means, what that relationship could be, incorporating degrees of obsessive, even aggressive, extremes and transgressions."[1] When they are asked why they use video for their works, they reply that this is because video is so immediate and allows them to see directly and control what they are doing. Elsewhere in the conversation they point out that they are investigating the possibility of live performances, and in fact do not view themselves as video artists. Yet video is not just a medium that is particularly handy or easy to use for exploring a male/female relationship. On the contrary, the acuity of Smith/Stewart's work may well derive from the fact that they in effect overlay the video connection of image and subject with the connection between a man and a woman: in these works video functions as a *metaphor* for the male/female relationship.

The crucial point is, as the artists themselves indicate in the cited conversation, the immediacy of video. A video-image shares essential characteristics with the mirror-image: it is present on the monitor in the moment when the subject steps in front of the camera. Even if, unlike a mirror, the video holds out the possibility of delaying the replay as opposed to the recording, nevertheless every video image is impregnated with the real-time bond between the image and videoed subject, and vice versa.

[1] Stephanie Smith and Edward Stewart in conversation with Kim Sweet, in: *Smith/Stewart, Sustain*, The Showroom, 22 November – 17 December 1995, unpaginated

This bond is realised by the gaze. The gaze binds the two together and the subject is caught up in a compelling feedback relationship, without history and without difference. Because of this immediacy, Rosalind Krauss defines *narcissism* as the actual medium of video, rather than the relevant electronic equipment.[2]

The immediacy of this relationship means that – as long as the *reflective* relationship of the subject and its image is maintained by the gaze – there is no possibility of establishing that dependence of the portrayal on the portrayed, which is at the root of the pictorial theory of the metaphysical tradition, and of escaping from dependence on the portrayal. Nothing can save Narcissus: "Stretched on the grassy shade he gazes down on the false phantom, staring endlessly, his eyes his own undoing" – as Ovid describes it. And when the picture becomes clouded because his tears have disturbed the calm of the surface of the water, the lover pleads: "Oh, cruelty to leave your lover so! Let me but gaze on what I may not touch and feed the aching fever in my heart."[3] Narcissus' delusion is fatal, for he clings to the visual relationship which chains him to his image: his desire is coupled in perfect, inescapable symmetry to the desire of the (imaginary) Other. According to Lacan, no release can be expected through rational recognition of this visual relationship, since the "function of the I" itself derives from a failure to recognise which holds the subject in "imaginary servitude." In the "mirror stage" the formation of the 'I' occurs as identification with one's own mirror image – the image of the Other. From this point onwards the 'I' is filled with discord, which is a source of lasting frustration. "Thus, to break out of the circle of the *Innenwelt* [inner world] into the *Umwelt* [outer world] generates the inexhaustible quadrature of the ego's verification [récolements du *moi*]."[4] The task of psychoanalysis is to break through this mechanism. It "may accompany the patient to the ecstatic limit of the *'Thou art that'*, in which is revealed to him the cipher of his mortal destiny..."[5] Lacan indicates the path that should be taken: "...the art of the analyst must be to suspend the subject's certainties until their last mirages have been consumed. And it is in the discourse that the progress of their resolution must be marked."[6] Thus by entering the "field of speech and language" psychoanalysis shows the way out of the enslavement imposed by the gaze and the image.

With neither the capacity nor the urge to subject Smith/Stewart's work to psychoanalytic scrutiny, it is nevertheless fair to say that with their works they have been investigating the conditions of narcissistic identity which are realised in the visual perameters of video. Before Stephanie Smith and Edward Stewart began to collaborate in 1993, their work as

[2] Cf. Rosalind Krauss, 'Video: The Aesthetics of Narcissism, in: October 1, 1976, pp. 51ff.

[3] Publius Ovidus Naso, Metamorphoses, Book III, Oxford University Press, 1986, cited from: Barbara Bloom, *The Reign of Narcissism*, Württembergischer Kunstverein Stuttgart et al., 1990, pp. 51, 52

[4] Jacques Lacan, 'The mirror stage as formative of the function of the I', in: idem, *Écrits. A Selection*, transl. from the French by Alan Sheridan, London 1977, p. 4

[5] Op. cit., p. 7

[6] Idem, 'Function and field of speech and language in psychoanalysis', in: idem, op. cit., p. 43

individuals had already been marked by an interest in language.[7] In their pieces together, however, they explore relationships of representation, without leaving the field of the visual.

Their collaborative work is in most cases characterised by the duality of the performers. It has variously been pointed out, however, that their differences – above all their gender difference – is usually barely identifiable. *Gag* (1996) consists of a double projection: each of the two images shows a considerably enlarged section of face, covered with a coloured cloth which is then stuffed by the fingers or the tongue (of the other) into the mouth underneath it, until that mouth in the end is filled by the cloth and the face lies bare, which also allows the gender to be identified. The projections show the same thing happening side by side, as it turns out, in a reversal of male and female roles, an uncoordinated duplication of an act which one does to the other. Similarly, in *Breathing Space* (1997) the same situation is shown in two projections, parallel and unconnected. In this case, however, each screen only shows one performer, with her/his head in a plastic bag, which hides the face throughout the entire length of the video. They breathe inside the plastic bags, always close to suffocation, at one moment there is a panic-stricken intake of breath. Any differences between the two images are largely aesthetic, as in the different colours of the materials used by the two performers. The subjects are linked to each other, not by mutual reactions, but by symmetry (aside from some details) which gives them the appearance of mirror images: What one does, the other does – what one does to the other, one suffers from the other. Each is caught up in their own doing (actively or passively). "What am I looking at? Am I actually witnessing a very private, highly aestheticized auto-erotic ritual?", wonders one critic at the sight of *Breathing Space*.[8]

There is also a structural symmetry, albeit using different narratives – between *Dead Red* (1994) and part of *Sustain* (1995): he covers her body with kiss marks (from lipsticked lips), she covers his body with lovebites (mouth-made bruises).

In *Dual* (1997), a work shown on only one screen, the two performers are specifically involved in a seemingly mirrored act which directly raises the issue of their identity: her left hand is positioned above his left hand, while his right is positioned above her right hand in such a way that their lower arms are parallel. With his writing hand, he (right-handed) guides her non-writing hand, with her writing hand she (left-handed) guides his non-writing hand. With his hand, she writes his name, with her hand, he writes her name, again and again in the same place, so that the actual writing soon looks like an indecipherable tangle of lines. Each one's own

[7] I am not familiar with these early works. However, it is notable that various writers have commented on Smith/Stewart's interest in language without specifying any effect this may have had on their subsequent development.

[8] Iwona Blazwick, Polymorphous Perversity, Anthony d'Offay Gallery, 23 October — 27 November 1997, unpaginated

A Talk

(performed in writing)

Ulrich Loock: What is the function of pain in your works, as far as it plays a role in the interaction of the two performers? There seem to be different ways of integrating the notion of pain in some of the works, for instance pain that is not visually represented in a work but plays a role as a fact of common knowledge – the love bites in *Sustain*, as opposed to visual signifiers of pain in a work like *Interference*, where the action as such is not seen as responsible for that apparent pain.

Edward Stewart: I don't think there is pain in the work, certainly not depicted, discomfort maybe. Hopefully this discomfort is psychological – for both us and the viewer. We use sound to help stress this, without the sound there would be very little discomfort at all.

Stephanie Smith: I don't think that we intentionally use pain, but if it is implied, we have done this either through action *or* reaction, as you say. The (implied) pain is to elicit some bodily identification from the viewer – like the love bites in *Sustain* and the inflamed skin of the scratch pieces.

I suppose we see this more in terms of our endurance and "roles", ie. power relations which can change, be simultaneous or individual.

The "pain" you refer to in *Interference* is in the reaction shots which show our discomfort at being shouted at directly into the head (more especially ears). The viewer only sees our flinches, they do not hear the sound as

name, the signature of their identity, is written as an inscription by the other, and only for a moment – before they dissolve into illegibility – are the two names distinct from each other. The semblance of interaction soon proves to be a blurring of mutual identification.

Thus several of their works construe the relationship of the one to the other as a form of duplication, a male/female relationship along the lines of narcissism. In this sense the relationship realised between the two people – the content of the video-image – is precisely that same relationship which exists as the inescapable connection between video-image and subject. The visual parameters of video are reproduced in a relationship between two people. This connection is all the more significant in that the action in a work such as *Gag* is highly sexualised. It consists of an unmistakably phallic, yet not gender-specific, image of penetration that can be carried out and tolerated by either sex. The same might even be said of *Intercourse*, an earlier work (1993): one image shows a male mouth collecting saliva, while the other image shows this spit being caught by an open, female mouth. Even if this image of aggressive ejaculation and compliant acceptance maintains the apparently natural status quo, at the same time, here too the configuration of the projected images is so symmetrical that a reversal of the situation is more than just a distant possibility.

On the other hand, *Mouth to Mouth* (1995) – realised again in another version for *Sustain* (1995) – may be seen as a direct reference to the Narcissus legend, which, in its role as the creation myth of painting, has repeatedly been depicted throughout history. The man lies under water, and as soon as rising air-bubbles show that he is running out of air, the woman bends down into the water to blow her own breath into his lungs. Without hesitating, she breaks through the mirror-like surface of the water, the other proves not to be an image that dissipates when the reflective surface of the water is disturbed, but as an Other in vital need of help in the form of a donation of someone else's breath, which is then successfully administered. This narcissistic situation, the precursor of death in the myth, is the preserver of life in *Mouth to Mouth*. Yet the process of going below the surface of the water has no finality, it provides no actual release from the specular bond, because – in order to draw breath herself again – she must go back to the other side again, and is forced back into the visual relationship: of necessity her gaze is directed without interruption at the other under the water in order not to miss the inevitable moment when he will run out of breath again. There is no avoiding the compulsion to repeat breaking through the mirror, and as the

we heard it – this is because the microphones are placed in our mouths and therefore pick up the noise very differently. We're interested in this seeming disjuncture between sound and image and the relation between live and recorded. *Interference* seems uncomfortable or difficult to watch because of its intensity and pace. This urgency is open to connotations and has been read as both violent and sexual; it veers between hurting or overpowering someone and passionately kissing or smothering them – someone even remarked that it looked like we were giving one another electric shocks.

There is also implied pain in *Vent* through sound – the relentless screams are somewhere between a cry and a breath.

ES: Yes, and because of being positioned inside the body, the viewer internalises the sound as well.

More generally: what is the function in your works of extreme, aggressive, code-breaking ways of relating to each other?

ES: Good question. We sometimes show "intimate actions", but use cropping/framing to take away the specific context of the act. As a consequence of this – and by showing them in public – they become extreme and aggressive, or signify aggression – but at the same time they talk about intimacy, caring, desire and love.

SS: It's love! It's to heighten intensity and physicality. Anyway, our relations aren't solely aggressive – there is the nurturing side of *Sustain* (underwater) alongside the love bites. *Dead Red* started from wanting to kiss someone all over, which then turned into an obsessive, possessive marking.

Things may get aggressive as we are interested in disorientation, pushing extremes and the "in-between". Our early works were consensual but about testing out each other's trust, aggression was an inevitable element.

At some point you have objected to being positioned as video artists. You have even talked about the (theoretical) possibility of doing live performances. As far as I know, however, you have never done it. What is your reason for continuing to use video as the medium of your work?

ES: We were interested in live performance because we wanted to bring the viewer even closer – to make them a part of the work. Of course, we've always seen our work as being a very physical experience for the viewer, but we were becoming interested in the differences between our actual experience of making the work (eg. being underwater waiting for air, unable to see or hear clearly / being in plastic bags, sweating and panicking, trying to focus etc.) and how we showed it. This raised some interesting questions for us – we were interested in the viewer getting that

other in turn repeatedly becomes the image on the other side of the mirror again (the man underwater has his eyes open just as she must have) – the bond between the two holds fast as the "knot of imaginary servitude that love must always undo again, or sever" (Lacan). And the psychoanalyst adds: "For such a task, we place no trust in altruistic feeling, we who lay bare the aggressivity, that underlies the activity of the philanthropist, the idealist, the pedagogue, even the reformer."[9]

However, in several of the works by Smith/Stewart the aggressivity, that accompanies that altruistic feeling, the mask of narcissism, carves out its own course, as much in the 'phallic' works, *Intercourse* and *Gag*, as in the 'oral' works, *Dead Red* and *Sustain*. Pain, inflicted by direct, violent contact with the other's body, infiltrates the visual relationship. If we are to take covertly aggressive altruism as a sign of a narcissistic relationship to the Other, then the physical aggression in these pieces may be seen as the attempt to dissolve this imaginary bond and, by means of pain, to realise the fleshly, sensitive body of the Other, which is immersed in the same world as one's own body. Yet this pain is beyond the threshold of the visible, there is no place for it in the images themselves and it is not represented as such. It could be that the comment by the artists, cited at the opening of this essay, in which they refer to their interest in the possibilities of live performances, is a reaction to precisely this element of medial reduction.

In fact Smith/Stewart deal with the narcissistic situation by endeavouring to escape their visual relationship and to strip the eye of its status as the dominant sense organ. One of their latest pieces, *Inside Out* (1997), is different from all their other works in that it does not comprise the duality of the performers that had previously been obligatory. On a dark monitor a slit of light gradually opens up until it has become an almond-shape and the exhibition space itself is light, only to sink back into darkness as the opening closes again, and so on. The image shows the view from the back of the oral cavity looking outwards, as one can tell from the teeth and lips framing the light. The camera in the mouth takes on the role of the retina, the mouth gains sight and replaces the eye, it even looks like an eye.

In the majority of the videos, the fact is that the mouth is inserted into the visual relationship with the other, mouth-to-body or mouth-to-mouth. In works such as *Sustain* and *Dead Red* the camera-angle and the direction of the mouth moving towards the other's body are largely similar. Yet at the same time it is always clear that the oral connection is determined by its visual counterpart. The kiss marks, bruises and traces of lipstick are

[9] Cf. note 4, p. 7

close to our experience. However, we feel some of our most recent work has achieved this anyway, physically and psychologically, especially *Inside Out, Vent* and *Interference*.

ss: **Still working with video seems most appropriate to us. We're interested in the potentials of live performance but the right situation hasn't come up. We want to push the relationship between live and recorded but maybe not through a live piece, as this is now happening in the video works themselves. We are not "in opposition" to live performances, but we were trying to incorporate possibilities *into* video.**

We're also interested in using film, photography, sound – and space – in relation to specific ideas. We are not bound to video but choose to use whatever makes sense practically and conceptually in relation to our investigations.

In 1995 you stated, "we're really exploring a male/female relationship". Is this still true for your most recent works like *Inside Out* or *Vent*?

es: **Only in as far as we're in a male/female relationship – the intimacy involved in that relationship enables us to do certain things in the work and is inevitably reflected in it. I suppose that original quote was about exploring the politics of intimate relationships generally – but practically, through our own.**

ss: **Our work comes out of this – it's an inescapable fact! – but our ideas have moved on and it is no longer necessarily "subject matter". The male/female relationship does not have to be specific – it can talk about any intimate relations. Our work is hopefully more universal than being about us.**

Our work now is more concerned with the corporeal; the works you mention (ie. *Inside Out* and *Vent*) deal with the notion/experience/physicality of the body (male or female, personal or generic). So, there has been a shift.

What is the theoretical position of the video camera in the works where you take it inside your body, in order to film from the inside out – as opposed to its position in previous works where it seemed to coincide with the gaze of one of the performers or of a third party?

es: **We have used the camera both as an intermediary and as one of us. We still use the camera like this. Putting the camera/mic in the body puts the viewer "inside" us/themselves and thus, part of the work (as previously mentioned in relation to performance).**

ss: **Positioning the camera inside the body to look out, aims to provoke a direct physical response from the audience. The body itself frames the image.**

above all visible, and the penetration by the finger stuffing the material into a mouth may be seen as an image of the phallic character of the male gaze. Now, however, in *Inside Out*, the mouth returns this gaze. Now the mouth is no longer – as in other works – situated in the line of vision, but has itself become the source of the gaze. Through the mouth there is white light to be seen, the white of the light, no forms, no 'objectifying' – and as chance would have it, at this point I find myself leafing through Luce Irigaray's slim volume of *Elemental Passions*, and straight away, on page 7, come across the following: "White. Immense spaces. White, a rush of breath. Be swift, marry this breath. Remain in it. Make haste. Let it not abandon me. Let me not turn from it. Be swept up: my song. / You give me a blank white mouth. My white mouth, open, like an angel in a cathedral. You have stopped my tongue. What remains is song. I can say nothing but sing. / A song, for you. But that 'for you' is not a dative. Nor that song, a gift. Not received from you, not produced by me, nor for you, that song: my love with you. Intermingled. Escapes from me. A cloud... "[10] The gaze seated inside the mouth is different from the one we think we see visualised in the finger poking into the mouth. It does not objectify, it does not identify, it is all-encompassing, bound up in the world, bodily.

Breathing Space is the work in which the two performers, separately from each other and parallel to each other do the same as each other, just one thing, breathing inside a plastic bag. They struggle for breath, and gasp by gasp overcome the impossibility of breathing. Several of Smith/Stewart's other works also deal with breathing or are determined by breathing, even if this is not explicitly their subject matter. Breathing fulfils a variety of functions. It is the business of the mouth, the sigh of the spirit, which spreads out and fills the space, air connecting the interior and the exterior of the body, constantly – until its final and irrevocable interruption – travelling in both directions, not focused like the gaze. The introduction of breathing leads to the relativisation, if not to the replace-ment, of the eye. Breathing also marks out our actions, the very course of our lives, into regular rhythms. Thus, for example, while we have seen the compulsive repetition of the act in *Mouth to Mouth* as evidence of some psychic motive, a narcissistic bond – just when the mirror is broken through – breathing puts that repetition onto a natural, physical footing.

Very few of Smith/Stewart's videos are without sound (*Dead Red* is an exception, and certainly the most 'visual' of their pieces). The sound is usually loud and fills the exhibition space. It envelops the recipient and draws him or her into the work, in several works it is the sound of breathing. It is connected with the breathing of the viewer. Like those

[10] Luce Irigaray, *Elemental Passions*, New York 1992

The idea of being "inside" the head is not just due to the camera position though – but equally importantly, in how the installation space functions. We are equally interested in the other camera positions you mention, especially the gaze of the third party, which again relates directly to the viewer. In *Breathing Space* there are implications in looking down over someone, and the same in *Black Out* – the hand-held camera even picks up the motion of the other/camera-persons' breathing – this "other" is indeed also the (first) viewer.

We have also started to work with moving cameras as opposed to the often static camera of previous works. This can make the work less voyeuristic and thus the viewer is more implicated/involved – not a mere spectator.

What is the function of the white (light) in works like *Inside Out* or *Vent* (the absence of an image in a certain way)?

ss: The white light is the infinite, the void and about seeing. In *Inside Out* and *Vent* the image is stripped down to fundamentals – one doesn't need to see an image – the darkness/light, mouth, teeth are enough. The important thing is how this light works in the installation space – especially in relation to *Inside Out*, where the light illuminates an escape route. When the mouth is closed, the room is plunged into total darkness (and silence), one has to wait for the light/breath to be able to see (and get out).

In *Vent* the sound is important. The whiteness fills the entire end wall and becomes a screen of light. The (grey) teeth which enter from the top and bottom edges are the visual clues as to the source of the sound – the voice being expelled/directed outwards into the open space outside of/beyond the body. Relentlessly.

ES: "Absence of image", that's interesting, we don't see our work in terms of just the image, as in the projected image. The "image" is what you experience through the position you're put in by the camera, the sound of the piece and from the space of the installation itself.

Inside Out and *Vent* are about inside and out – you don't need another image.

How do you conceive the relation of sound and image in your recent works (sound now seems to be more independent from image than before)?

ss: Sound is always crucial for us (and conversely, silence). It is always the real sound and usually amplified. This is still the case, although sound is becoming something else (a little more "disjointed" perhaps) through the way it is being recorded eg. mics inserted into the body for *Interference* and *White Noise*, which cause distortion to occur. We're interested in pushing this in relation to the image and also in maybe

whose images I am seeing, I also breathe. The difference between seeing and hearing means that I do not perceive the recorded sound as a reproduction to the same extent that I view a visual image as such.

With the sound of breathing a third party becomes involved, who takes up a very different position to that of a viewer. The recipient sees what the camera has recorded. Basically the view of the recipient is also that of the camera, his or her ideal position coincides with the angle of the shot. At the same time, double projections serve, not least, to question the unity of the standpoint, relieving the recipient of the obligation to establish one, single viewing position. In this sense, videos where the camera angle coincides with the angle of vision of one of the performers should be distinguished from those where the camera takes up a documentary stance and frames a scene independently of the movements of the performers. In the first case the action is staged so that the narcissistic relationship between the performers (and the recipient) on the one hand and the image on the other hand is in keeping with the nature of video, while in other cases the recipient remains a viewer looking in from the outside.

In *Breathing Space*, the videoed, identical actions of the performers shown on two projections have been completely separated from each other. The mirror-effect remains un-reflected, a kind of blind narcissism. It is the recipient who hears the sounds of the two breathing and who in turns hears this together with his or her own breathing.[11] Through the breathing the recipient creates a link between the doubled images. Unlike the visual similarity, this link establishes a deep-rooted, physical individuality for the performers, which also acts as a foil for the recipient's own physical individuality. Thus it seems that the function of the enveloping sound is to involve a third party (who cannot simply be reduced to the viewer) with the performers – although this dimension of involvement is only available to the recipient. The involvement of the third party – seeing and hearing, breathing – heralds the demise of the specular relationship in favour of the actual co-existence of real bodies in a physical world: it is the third party who experiences the pain not represented in – excluded from – the videos. At the same time, due respect is still paid to the insurmountable distance and the inevitable closeness inherent in the visual parameters of video. The images are projected directly onto the wall of the exhibition space: the wall becomes the projection screen. This immediacy in Smith/Stewart's work suggests a future direction their journey may take.

What makes Smith/Stewart's work significant is the rigour with which they realise the reflective relationship of image and subject (which is

[11] Cf. my text 'Breathing Space. The Third One as Medium', in: exh. cat., *Glasgow*, Kunsthalle Bern 1997

letting the sound become something in itself (totally independent perhaps).

ES: I wouldn't say it's more independent. We still use the real sound of our actual recordings, even in *Interference* – we are just recording sound from a different perspective, using the body as an intermediary for sound. We do this to again play with the viewer's relationship to the act through the disjuncture between sound and image.

The relation between mouth and eye, going as far as intimating the replacement of one for the other, seems to be one of the most fundamental structures of your work. How do you conceive this relation?

SS: This relationship has evolved. We have used the mouth as a way of exploring, of looking almost and the camera as a way of making visible, of seeing.

The title of our recent Fruitmarket show was *Hooded.Bared* (from Beckett's *Company*), which describes the eyelid opening and closing. (It also held many other readings for us.) The closest, most apparent relation between mouth and eye is an *Inside Out* where the mouth becomes an eye.

The mouth/eye structure also talks of the relationship of language and the visual.

ES: It's the closest we can get to using the body as an aperture; looking out. The mouth has always been important – it's the beginning and the end (especially in relation to breath). It's a communicator both pre-verbally and through language.

One of the most important, and most recurrent features in your work is breath (image, sound). What is the function of breathing and what are your references in making breath this important an issue?

SS: It's a fundamental action! – and of the body. We have made it both visible and audible – identifiable – by bringing attention to it in various ways. The function of breath for us is to make the viewer aware of their own body, their own breath – they become a participant, "The Third One as Medium".

Breath measures time, it can go to extremes (suffocation, breathlessness). It can be regular or reach crescendos. Our breaths can go in and out of sync – together and apart.

You can relate breath to yourself and/or an other.

Breath can be life-saving.

We are interested in the relationship between breath and spit – that it is bound up with the body and its functions.

It talks of mortality, presence and absence.

intrinsic to the nature of video) in a male/female relationship. No doubts regarding the power of this relationship are permitted. Smith/Stewart extend the disunity which initially characterises the 'I' – the "stadium" of a fortified place[12] – into the parallel side-by-sidedness and oppositeness of two people. These two people are identifiable as man and woman, although their reflective relationship disperses any fixed notions of gender. In the interior of the "stadium" they take advantage of the possibilities of spatialisation in order to shift their relationship to each other, introducing the mouth into the visual relationship, until the mouth itself in fact gains sight. But with this exploration of their own relationship they also shift the relationship between the image and the subject of the video. One might say that with that "stadium" Smith/Stewart have created a new place for the 'spectator' whose bodily integration into the spatially installed work – above all immersed in the sound of the breathing, and breathing along with that sound – reconstructs the reality of those other bodies which are no more than images in the video.

[12] Lacan (as in note 4, p. 5) writes: "Correlatively, the formation of the *I* [formation du *je*] is symbolized in dreams by a fortress, or a stadium – its inner arena and enclosure, surrounded by marshes and rubbish-tips, dividing it into two opposed fields of contest where the subject flounders in quest of the lofty, remote inner castle whose form (sometimes juxtaposed in the same scenario) symbolizes the *id* in a quite startling way. Similarly, on the mental plane, we find realized the structures of fortified works, the metaphor of which arises spontaneously, as if issuing from the symptoms themselves, to designate the mechanisms of obsessional neurosis – inversion, isolation, reduplication, cancellation and displacement." The French word 'stade' implies both spatial and temporal limitations: translated in this passage as 'stadium,' it can also be translated as 'stage' (see the title of this essay by Lacan, as in note 4).

It is an ongoing rhythm/pulse both before and beyond language.

It is something that is always there.

ES: We're very interested in darkness. Deprived of light and without sound, you start to hear other sounds – your own.

Through our work/"performances" we become aware of our own breath, often through the other's, and have attempted to visualise what normally isn't seen.

Der Portikus Frankfurt am Main dankt der Kultur-Stiftung der Deutschen Bank, Berlin, für die Unterstützung der Ausstellung

KULTUR-STIFTUNG

Deutsche Bank Gruppe ☑